Countries We Come From

Germany

by Jessica Rudolph

Consultant: Karla Ruiz, MA
Teachers College, Columbia University
New York, New York

BEARPORT PUBLISHING

New York, New York

Credits

Cover, © Africa Studio/Shutterstock and © Whatafoto/Shutterstock; TOC, © Thomas Vogel/iStock; 4, © canadastock/Shutterstock; 5T, © FamVeld/Shutterstock; 5B, © canadastock/Shutterstock; 7, © Meinzahn/iStock; 8, © imageBROKER/Alamy; 9T, © canadastock/Shutterstock; 9B, © seewhatmitchsee/iStock; 10, © Neil Burton/Shutterstock; 11T, © Christopher MacDonald/Shutterstock; 11B, © Florian Andronache/Shutterstock; 12, © "Frederick II (1712–86) the Great" (oil on canvas), French School, (18th century)/Musee Conde, Chantilly, France/Bridgeman Images; 13, © canadastock/Shutterstock; 14L, © INTERFOTO/Alamy; 14R, © Chronicle/Alamy; 15, © VitalyEdush/iStock; 16, © Iain Masterton/Alamy; 17, © Leonardo Patrizi/iStock; 18–19, © querbeet/iStock; 19B, © Leonardo Patrizi/iStock; 20T, © amlet/Shutterstock; 20B, © lightstock/iStock; 21, © imageBROKER/Alamy; 22, © Alizada Studios/Alamy; 23, © Karl Allgaeuer/Shutterstock; 24, © AMzPhoto/iStock; 25, © Smileus/iStock; 26T, © PARIS PIERCE/Alamy; 26B, © "Portrait of brothers Jacob and Wilhelm Grimm," 1855 (oil on canvas), Jerichau-Baumann, Elisabeth Maria Anna (1819–1881)/Alte Nationalgalerie, Berlin, Germany/De Agostini Picture Library/Bridgeman Images; 27T, © Lebrecht Music and Arts Photo Library/Alamy; 27B, © "Postcard depicting the witch inviting Hansel and Gretel to enter the gingerbread house," c.1910 (colour litho), German School, (20th century)/Private Collection/Archives Charmet/Bridgeman Images; 28–29, © Tumarkin Igor - ITPS/Shutterstock; 29R, © paul prescott/Shutterstock; 30T, © Viktor Kunz/Shutterstock and © spinetta/Shutterstock; 30BL, © Jagodka/Shutterstock; 30BR, © Eric Isselee/Shutterstock; 31 (T to B), © querbeet/Shutterstock, © Jagodka/Shutterstock, © Lebrecht Music and Arts Photo Library/Alamy, and © Boris Stroujko/Shutterstock; 32, © Aaron Amat/Shutterstock.

Publisher: Kenn Goin
Editor: J. Clark
Creative Director: Spencer Brinker
Photo Researcher: Thomas Persano

Library of Congress Cataloging-in-Publication Data

Names: Rudolph, Jessica, author.
Title: Germany / by Jessica Rudolph.
Description: New York, New York : Bearport Publishing Company, Inc., [2017] | Series: Countries we come from | Includes bibliographical references and index. | Audience: Ages 5–8.
Identifiers: LCCN 2016038806 (print) | LCCN 2016039034 (ebook) | ISBN 9781684020539 (library binding) | ISBN 9781684021055 (ebook)
Subjects: LCSH: Germany—Juvenile literature.
Classification: LCC DD17 .R83 2017 (print) | LCC DD17 (ebook) | DDC 943—dc23
LC record available at https://lccn.loc.gov/2016038806

For more information, write to Bearport Publishing Company, Inc., 45 West 21st Street, Suite 3B, New York, New York 10010. Printed in the United States of America.

10 9 8 7 6 5 4 3 2 1

Contents

This Is Germany

STUNNING

Friendly

HISTORIC

Germany is a large country in Europe.

More than 80 million people live there.

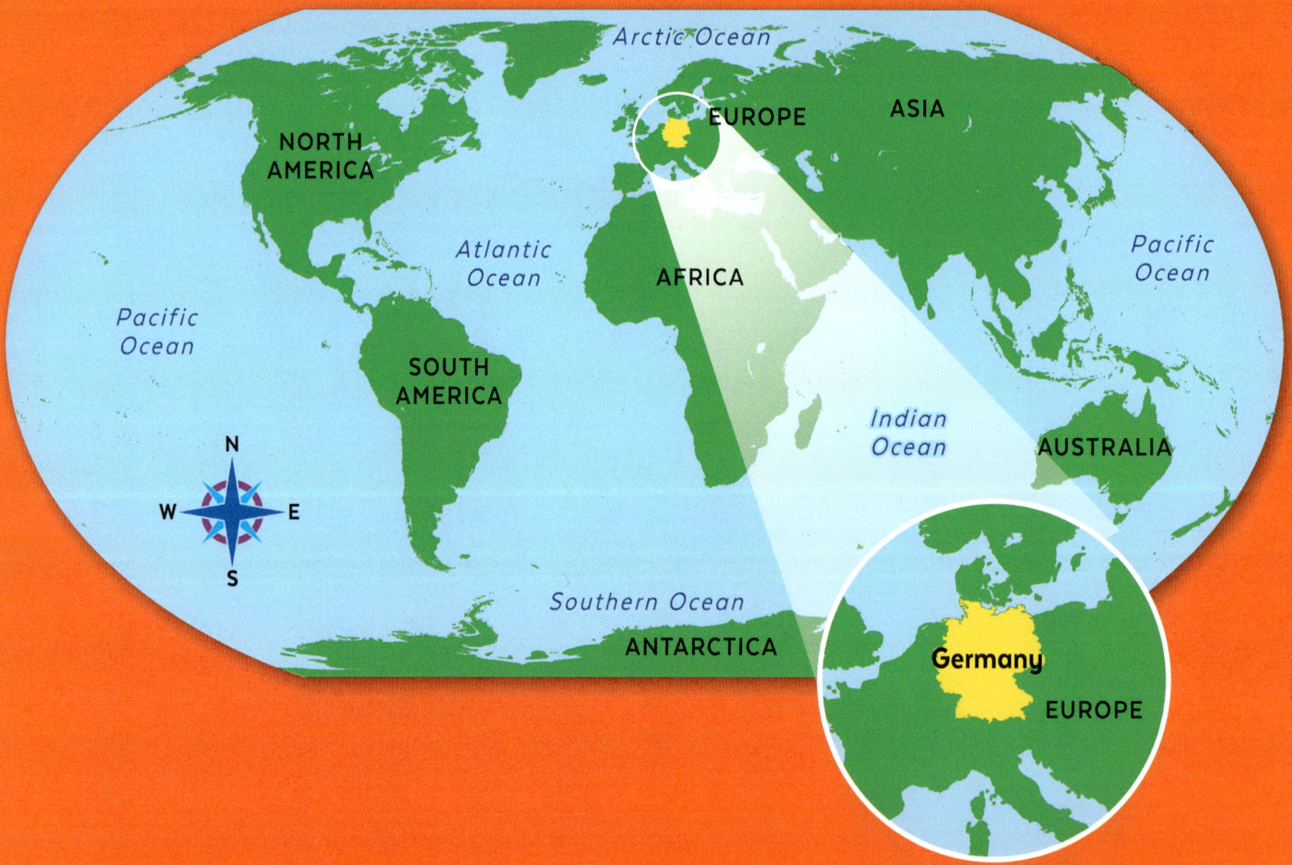

Germans call their country Deutschland (DOYTCH-land).

Germany has different types of land. Rivers wind through **plains**.

Mountains called the Alps rise high into the sky.

The Black Forest is in southern Germany. It's filled with tall evergreen trees.

Many amazing animals live in Germany.

Deer roam the countryside.

Pine martens dart from tree to tree.

Cuckoos also make their home in Germany. These birds are named for the call they make.

Long ago, Germany was made up of many small countries.

They were ruled by princes and kings.

In 1871, the small countries **united** to create one large country.

King Frederick the Great

The princes and kings lived in castles. Today, people can visit the old castles.

In the 1900s, nations around the world fought in two major wars.

Some battles were fought in Germany.

Many cities were bombed.

the bombed city of Dresden

After the wars, the German people rebuilt their cities.

modern-day Dresden

People in Germany speak German.

This is how you say *hello* in German:

Guten Tag (GOOT-en TAHK)

This is how you say *goodbye*:

Auf Wiedersehen (OWF VEE-dair-zayn)

Many words used in the English language are German, such as *kindergarten*.

The **capital** of Germany is Berlin.
It is also the country's largest city.

About 3.5 million people live in Berlin.

Germans have many types of jobs.

Some work on farms raising pigs and cows.

Farmers also grow **crops** such as apples.

Other people make cars in factories.

German cars are sold all over the world.

Germans make lots of delicious food.

One popular meal is sausage and sauerkraut (SOW-ur-krowt).

Sauerkraut is cabbage with a sour flavor.

For a treat, many Germans eat freshly baked pretzels.

Christmas is a big holiday in Germany.

People buy decorations and gifts at outdoor markets.

Many Christmas traditions, such as decorating trees, started in Germany.

Have you heard of "Little Red Riding Hood"?

This story is well known because of two German brothers.

Jacob and Wilhelm Grimm

In the 1800s, the Grimm brothers collected **fairy tales** and wrote them down in books.

Grimm's fairy tales also include "Cinderella" and "Hansel and Gretel."

Cinderella

Hansel and Gretel

What's the most popular sport in Germany?

Soccer!

People across the country play the sport.

In 2014, Germany won the World Cup. Countries all over the world play in this soccer competition.

Fast Facts

Capital city:
Berlin

Population of Germany:
More than 80 million

Main language:
German

Money: Euro

Major religion: Christianity

Neighboring countries include:
Poland, Austria, and France

Cool Fact: Many breeds of dogs were first raised in Germany, including German shepherds and Great Danes.

Glossary

capital (KAP-uh-tuhl) a city where a country's government is based

crops (KRAHPS) plants that are grown for food

fairy tales (FAIR-ee TAYLZ) children's stories about imaginary beings

plains (PLAYNZ) large, flat areas of land

united (yoo-NEYE-tid) joined together

Index

Read More

Blashfield, Jean F. *Germany (Enchantment of the World).* New York: Children's Press (2013).

Simmons, Walter. *Germany (Exploring Countries: Blastoff! Readers).* Minneapolis, MN: Bellwether Media (2011).

Learn More Online

To learn more about Germany, visit
www.bearportpublishing.com/CountriesWeComeFrom

About the Author

Jessica Rudolph is a writer from Connecticut. Some of her family members came to America from Hanover, in northern Germany, and Munich, in southern Germany, in the 1800s.